© Autumn Publishing Ltd 2003

A CIP catalogue record for this book is available from the British Library.

ISBN 1858547105 paperback
ISBN 1858546273 hardback

Printed in China

MONEY DOESN'T GROW ON TREES!

BRIMAX

First published by Brimax,
an imprint of Autumn Publishing Ltd,
Appledram Barns, Chichester PO20 7EQ

Created by Nimbus Books
Written by Lorraine Horsley
Illustrated by John Eastwood

Contents

Money, money, money

What is money and why do we need it? You might think money is not important, but without it we could not buy cars, televisions, computer games, magazines, or even sweets. We would not have food to eat, be able to go on holiday, go to the cinema, or buy birthday presents for our family and friends.

Earning money

Most people get money by working. Employers pay people to make things or do certain jobs, such as fixing cars, cutting hair, teaching children (someone has to do it!), or programming computers. Some jobs pay more money than others. A few lucky actors earn millions for appearing in films and on television. Other jobs you can do when you are still at school.

Inheriting money

This is when someone dies and leaves their money or belongings to a friend or member of their family.

A great idea

You could become a millionaire by coming up with an idea, or invention, that no one else has thought of. This could be something that saves people time, or that does the job of an existing machine but with better results. So keep up with those science lessons!

Top earners

Imagine getting paid lots of money to do something you enjoy, like playing sport. Successful sportspeople, such as golfers, can be among the world's highest earners. They earn money by playing sport, and also by endorsing products. This means companies pay them to wear certain clothes or use one brand of equipment. The companies hope this will encourage other people to wear or use these things, too.

Before money

Before money was invented, people grew their own food and made all the clothes, pots, and tools they needed. They built simple homes out of wood or earth. If they wanted something that they could not grow or make themselves, they would swap or trade with other people. This is called bartering. Once towns developed, people started to use money.

DID YOU KNOW?

Roman soldiers were sometimes paid in salt. This is where the word salary comes from, which means wages.

Funny money

In the past, people have used cloth, metals, and food as money.

Dried tea (Tibet)

Bamboo sticks (China)

Cocoa beans (Mexico)

Swap shop

You can still use the bartering system today. Why not swap some of your old toys or comics with your friends?

Sometimes the person you are trying to swap things with does not want anything that belongs to you. In this case you have to use money instead. Money can be any object, no matter how strange, so long as it is valuable to the person receiving it.

Wampum belts made from clam shells (North America)

Copper rings (Nigeria)

Tobacco (US)

In short supply

During the Second World War (1939–1945), Germany bombed the cargo ships that brought goods to the UK. This meant that luxury items, such as cigarettes, ladies' stockings, perfume, and sweets, were in very short supply and became valuable. People used to barter with these goods instead of money.

Modern money

Look in your piggy bank. Is it full of coins and banknotes? Hopefully, you have some money in there, but modern money is not just made of pieces of paper or metal discs. You can pay for things using credit cards or cheques. Some money you cannot even see or touch because it only exists as information in a computer.

Banknotes

Banknotes are printed on strong paper made from cotton (so money doesn't grow on trees, it grows on cotton plants!). The paper often has watermarks in it which can be seen when held up to the light. The pictures and letters on banknotes are cut into soft metal blocks called dies. The dies are used to make printing plates, which transfer ink onto paper.

Minting

Coins are made by stamping words and pictures onto blank pieces of metal. This is called minting.

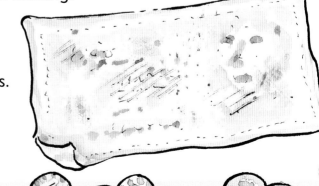

Fake money

Photocopying banknotes is illegal. To stop people from doing this, many banknotes contain plastic strips. In daylight these strips may look red or some other colour, but when photocopied they appear black.

Different ways to pay

Adults can buy things using credit cards. These cards have a magnetic strip that stores information about the customers, so the credit companies know where to find them when it is time to pay their bills! Grown-ups can also pay their bills over the telephone. This is called telephone banking.

Automatic Teller Machines (ATM)

Many banks have ATMs. These are computers which customers can use at any time, to draw out cash or find out how much money they have in the bank. To use an ATM you need a special plastic card and a secret number, called a PIN (Personal Identification Number). You will not get one of these until you are older, though.

Electronic money

Computers in banks and businesses hold lots of information about how much money you have. If you have access to the internet, you can send this information to other computers and pay your bills without leaving your desk.

Pocket money

Although it is great if your parents buy all your things for you, it is good to have money of your own so you can choose what you want to buy. Even the meanest of parents can be persuaded to give their children pocket money each week. The bad news is they will probably expect you to earn it by helping around the home!

Good earners

Parents will pay more pocket money for certain jobs. Here are some jobs you could do to earn money:

Loading or unloading the dishwasher
Cleaning around the house
Mowing the lawn
Cleaning a pet cage
Vacuuming
Taking out the rubbish
Laying the table
Making beds

Getting a raise

If you would like more pocket money, why not ask your parents if you can do extra jobs for them? You could offer to clean the goldfish bowl or wash the car, for example.

Budgeting

It is very tempting to spend all your pocket money as soon as you get it, but if you do, you will always be short of money. A better idea is to plan your weekly budget.

- Work out what you need to spend each week on things like comics or bus fares.
- Remember to keep some money for holidays or to buy birthday presents for your friends.
- If you want to buy something special, put aside a small amount of your pocket money each week to pay for it.
- Do not borrow money to pay for something. Wait until you have saved the money.

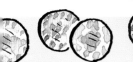

Bank accounts

Suppose you don't manage to spend all your pocket money, what do you do with the extra money? You could hide it under your bed – but a better idea might be to open a bank account. That way your money will be safe from your brother or sister, and you won't lose it. But the best thing about banks is they pay you extra money, called interest.

How to choose a bank

To help you pick the right bank, ask these questions:

- How much interest will the bank pay me?
- Is there a branch near my home?
- Is the bank open after school and at weekends?
- How much money do I need to deposit, or put in, to start my account?
- How much money can I withdraw, or take out, at one time?

Open sesame!

To open a bank account, you will need to fill in an application form. The bank needs to see some form of identification, such as your birth certificate. And don't forget – you'll need some money to put into your new account! Most banks give you a pass book. You will need to take this to the bank every time you want to put in or take out money. Banks send regular statements, which show how much money has been paid in or taken out of your account.

That's interesting

Banks pay you for allowing them to look after and use your money. The longer you leave your money with them, the more they pay you. It works like this: imagine that Piggy Bank pays 5% interest. If you save £100 for one year, the bank will give you £5.

Bank statement

PIGGY BANK

Sariya Hamilton

Account No. 325463247

Date	Deposit (+) / Withdrawal (-)	Balance
14 June	£2.50 +	£2.50
18 June	£1.25 -	£1.25
21 June	£3.00 +	£4.25
24 June	£1.00 -	£3.25
28 June	£3.65 +	£6.90
2 July	£2.00 +	£8.90
Interest payable	£0.25+	£9.15

Stocks and shares

One way to make your money grow is to buy and sell stocks and shares. Companies sell shares to raise money to improve their business. By buying shares, you will get to own a part of big companies such as Nike™ or Ford™. But before you get carried away, remember that millions of other people own shares, too, so you won't be in charge!

How shares work

If the company does well, the value of the shares increases and you can sell them for more than you paid. But if the value of the shares decreases, you will sell them for less than you paid.

Children's Bonus Bonds

A safe and steady way to save is by investing in Children's Bonus Bonds, available in units of twenty-five pounds. Designed as a long-term investment, the Bonds earn interest over a five-year period at a fixed rate. At the fifth anniversary a bonus is added, which is fixed and guaranteed from the start. After the five year period the Bond may be left invested and will continue to earn interest and further bonuses.

Stock markets

Stocks and shares are sold in places called stock markets or stock exchanges. The biggest stock exchanges are in London, New York, Tokyo, and Hong Kong.

You can find out the price of shares by reading the business section of daily newspapers or looking on the internet. The companies are grouped together according to what they make or sell. So in the retailers' section you will find shops.

This is the price of each share on a particular day.

RETAILERS

Funky Fashions   825p   + 2.5p

Casual Knits   725p   − 1.2p

This shows how much the price of the share has gone up (+) or down (−) during the day.

DID YOU KNOW?

Ray Kroc used to own the burger chain, McDonald's™. He lost £27 million pounds in just one day when the value of his shares fell! Poor man.

Be a city whizz kid

Do you think you could make money by buying and selling shares? Before you risk your own money, why not practise by playing a game of Virtual Stock Exchange? You can play this game on your own or with a friend. First, you will need to do some research to decide which companies you want to invest in, then you can play.

How to play

- Imagine you have £1,000. You can use all that money to buy shares in a single company, or you can buy a small number of shares in lots of different companies.
- Use the share prices in newspapers to help you choose (you might need an adult to check that you haven't overspent.)
- Set yourself a time limit of between one and three months. During this time you can buy and sell as many shares as you like. The more money you make during the game, the more shares you can buy.
- At the end of the game you must sell all your shares and add up how much money you have made (or lost!)

Helpful hints

- Check the value of your shares every day. If the price of your shares goes up, you might want to sell them to make money quickly. If the price falls, you can either sell your shares before you lose too much money or hang on to them and hope that the price goes up again before the end of the game.

- Choose some companies that you use yourself, such as your favourite clothes shop, music shop, or fast food restaurant. If you know the company is popular, the chances are that the company will do well and that the share price will go up.

- Try to find out what other companies sell or do. This will help you to guess if they are likely to do well. For instance, if you hear a weather forecaster say that there's going to be a cold, wet summer, it would be better to buy shares in a company that makes umbrellas, not one that makes ice cream!

Earning your own money

Now that you have had a chance to play the stock market, you might like to earn some real money of your own. Whatever you do, make sure your parents know what you are up to and where you are at all times. The best place to start is close to home. Ask your family and neighbours if they need any jobs doing.

Odd jobs

You can begin by doing jobs for your neighbours. They will probably be only too pleased to let you do those jobs they really hate, such as washing their cars or mowing their lawns.

Early riser?

When you are old enough to be allowed out early in the morning on your own, you could try to get a job delivering newspapers or leaflets. But be warned, this can be hard work, especially at the weekend, when the newspapers include lots of heavy magazines!

A way with animals

If your neighbours have a cat, you could offer to feed it while they are on holiday. Or, if your neighbours have a dog, you could take it for a walk.

Green fingers

If your neighbours do not have any pets, you could always offer to water their plants when they go on holiday. But remember, you will have to water them every day; it's not enough to drown them once a week!

Car booting

Why not hold a car boot or garage sale? By selling all your old toys you will make money. You will also get into your mum's good books by clearing out all the rubbish that's been lying around your bedroom for years. But be sure to sell only things that belong to you.

Start your own business

Some of the world's richest and most successful people started their businesses when they were the same age as you. All you need is a great idea and the ability to work hard. First, you need to decide what you are going to sell; a product or a service? If you enjoy making things, then it's probably best to make and sell a product.

Choose a theme

- Valentine's Day could be a perfect opportunity to make and sell products such as cards or cuddly toys.
- Christmas is a good time, too. How about making handmade wrapping paper? You could also offer a gift wrapping service.
- Summer is an ideal time to run a lawn-mowing service. You could cut your neighbours' lawns and water their plants.
- In the winter, you could offer to shovel snow from driveways, and scrape ice off car windscreens.

Seasonal work

You need to decide if you are going to run your business all year round, or just for certain months of the year. This is called seasonal work. If you offer a service, such as pet sitting, you will probably work mainly in the summer when people are on holiday. If you offer a car washing service, you will be able to work all year round.

Getting started

Think about the following before you start:

- How much will it cost you to buy the materials to make your product?
- Where will you get the money to pay for the materials? Parents? Savings?
- Who will make your product? If someone else is making it, how much will you have to pay them?
- Will people work for you? If so, how much will you pay them?
- How many items will you make?
- How long will this take?

25

Your customers

When you start to run your own business, you need to think carefully about the most important people in the world: your customers. Who are you going to sell to? Is it your friends and family or your neighbours? It is important to know who your customers are so you can choose the right product or service to offer.

Finding your customers

Where will you do your selling? Think about where your customers are and take your product or service to them. If you want to wash cars, knock on the doors of neighbours who own cars. You also need to tailor your product to your customers. If your neighbours are elderly, for example, they probably won't be interested in buying tie-dyed T-shirts!

Advertising

Don't forget to let people know about your business by advertising. If you are offering gardening or babysitting services, post notices through the doors of family and friends. Never approach strangers. You could be extra professional and make leaflets, but they can be expensive to print, so remember to add this cost into the price you charge for your product.

Dot and Dougal's Dog-walking
Do Pooch, Polly, and Bruno need walking?
We will walk your dogs for one hour each day.

Call Dougal on 54321

The internet

Some people use the internet to advertise their business. If you use the internet for this purpose, **always** tell your parents what you are doing!

Be reliable in business

You must never let your customers down. If you do, they will not trust you again. If you say you will collect Bruno at 9 am to take him for his morning walk, make sure you are there on time.

The competition

There is another group of people you need to get to know: your competitors. These are people or businesses who offer the same product or service as you. Try to find out as much as you can about your competitors, including how much they charge; what is good about their product or service; what is bad; why people buy their product or service.

Beating the competition

The next step is to think how you can beat the competition.

- Can you offer a product or service that is better in some way? Will your biscuits taste nicer, are your card designs cooler?
- Can you sell your product cheaper than your competitors? Check how much your product costs to make. There is no point selling things cheaply if you do not make a profit.

REMEMBER Profit = sales revenue − cost of materials − cost of advertising.

A unique product

One way to be successful in business is to sell something that your competitors do not make. For example, Clarence Birdseye. He was the first person to introduce frozen foods way back in 1925. His brand is still well-known today! Or, you could try to think of a way to improve an existing product to make your version better.

Branding

Coca Cola® is the most famous and bestselling brand in the world. Its nearest rival is Pepsi®. In order to compete with these two companies, supermarkets have to sell their own brand cola much cheaper. This shows how important it is to get a good reputation. If people really prefer your product, they will pay more for it.

Who wants to be a millionaire?

You do not have to be old to be rich. If you start your business now, who knows, one day you could own a huge corporation and employ lots of people. Then you will need to think about how to spend all your money! Here are a few examples of people who made their millions early on and what you might like to spend your money on.

Computer millions

Bill Gates started making computers when he was just 20 years old. By the time he was 30, he was a billionaire. He is now one of the world's richest people.

TV star millions

Some of the richest people in the world are film stars and models. People at the top of their careers can earn millions for making one film or appearing in one advertising campaign. But remember, for most of these people, it wasn't just talent, they were also very lucky.

Don't be mean

Hetty Green was one of the world's richest women. But she was so mean that she ate cold porridge so she did not have to spend money heating it up!

How to spend your millions

When you are a millionaire, you will need help to spend all your money.

Why not treat your mum to some nice jewellery? Unless you are really rich you will not be able to afford the world's most expensive diamond. This was sold in 1995 for £10,507,143!

Even if you are not old enough to drive, you could buy a new car for your dad. Why not spoil him with an Aston Martin sports car. It will cost you around £150,000, but it will make your dad happy! In the meantime, you could buy him a model sports car until you make your millions!

How about having a party for all your friends and family? The world's most expensive party was held on 13 July, 1976, in Brunei. It cost an amazing £17 million!

Glossary

Advertisement
A way of letting your customers know what you are selling. Advertisements appear in magazines, on billboards, and on the radio and television.

Balance
The difference between the money you put into the bank (deposit) and what you take out (withdraw).

Bartering
Trading without using money by swapping things that others want.

Budget
A plan of how much money you have and how you will spend it.

Competition
The other people or companies who sell a similar product or service to yours.

Credit card
A card that allows you to buy things without using money.

Customer
The people who buy your product or service.

Deposit
Placing money into a bank account.

Employee
A person who works for someone or a company in return for a salary.

Employer

A person or company that pays someone money in return for their work.

Endorsing

Expressing approval for a product or company.

Interest

Money a bank pays its customers for letting them look after and use their money.

Minting

Making coins by stamping discs of metal.

Profit

How much money you make from selling a product after you have subtracted how much it has cost to make.

Salary

The money or wages paid by employers to their workers for doing a job.

Shares

Equal parts of a company. Each part has the same value.

Stock exchange

A place where shares in companies can be bought and sold.

Withdrawal

Removal of money from a bank account.